CHINA-JAPAN-U.S.

The Japan Center for International Exchange wishes to thank

The Nippon Foundation

Asia Pacific Agenda Project

The Ford Foundation

CHINA-JAPAN-U.S.

Managing the
Trilateral Relationship

Morton I. Abramowitz
Funabashi Yoichi
Wang Jisi

with an introduction by
Yamamoto Tadashi

Tokyo • Japan Center for International Exchange • *New York*

Copyediting by Pamela J. Noda.
Cover and typographic design by Becky Davis, EDS Inc.,
Editorial & Design Services. Typesetting and production by EDS Inc.

Printed in Japan
ISBN 4-88907-016-8

Distributed worldwide outside Japan by Brookings Institution Press,
1775 Massachusetts Avenue, N.W., Washington, D.C. 20036-2188 U.S.A.

Japan Center for International Exchange
9-7 Minami Azabu 4-chome, Minato-ku, Tokyo 106 Japan

URL: http://www.jcie.or.jp

Japan Center for International Exchange, Inc. (JCIE/USA)
1251 Avenue of the Americas, New York, N.Y. 10020 U.S.A.

Contents

Is a China-Japan-U.S. Trilateral Dialogue Possible?

Yamamoto Tadashi

WHILE THE EMERGING ASIA PACIFIC REGION will have a profound impact on the future of the international system, there is a growing awareness that the continuing security and prosperity of the region will be largely contingent upon enhanced cooperation between the region's three dominant economies: China, Japan, and the United States. Such consciousness has been enhanced by the end of the cold war and the disappearance of the common threat to the three countries—the Soviet Union—as well as by the rapid economic development of China with concomitant growth of its political influence in the Asia Pacific region and beyond.

A joint research and dialogue project on the China-Japan-U.S. trilateral relationship was conceived by several individuals in the three countries who believed that promoting analysis and dialogue among them would be critical and essential in managing the trilateral relationship. After repeated consultations and careful planning over more than one year, the Japan Center for International Exchange, in collaboration with the Institute of American Studies of the Chinese Academy of Social Sciences and the Chinese Reform Forum on the Chinese side and the Carnegie Endowment for International Peace on the U.S. side, launched a trilateral joint project in December 1996 with a workshop in Beijing attended by leading policy thinkers from the three countries. The three essays in this volume were prepared as background papers for the Beijing workshop by the leaders of the project: Wang Jisi, director of the

Institute of American Studies and a leading international relations specialist in China; Funabashi Yoichi, chief diplomatic correspondent and columnist for the *Asahi Shimbun*, a large Japanese daily newspaper, who has been stationed in Beijing and as bureau chief in Washington, D.C.; and Morton I. Abramowitz, a former diplomat and recently retired president of the Carnegie Endowment for International Peace who is now a senior fellow at the Council on Foreign Relations. The papers were revised for publication after the Beijing workshop to reflect the very active interactions among the participants.

CHALLENGES TO
CHINA-JAPAN-U.S. TRILATERAL RELATIONS

While the three authors of this volume as well as some others involved in launching the China-Japan-U.S. Research and Dialogue Project felt the need for trilateral dialogue, they also felt that there should be a clearer understanding of what that trilateral relationship constitutes and why it is important. As Abramowitz writes, "Some feel the 'trilateral relationship' is a new imperative, though no one has actually defined it." Yet, as Wang recognizes, "It is sensible and justifiable to study China-Japan-U.S. relations from a trilateral perspective, as each bilateral connection within the three influences, and is influenced by, the third party's behavior." Funabashi also recognizes that "trying to deal with each bilateral relationship separately from the others is almost completely unworkable. More and more, each bilateral relationship will become ensnared in the trilateral relationship as a whole."

In launching this project, it was decided that we should try to develop a better understanding of the nature of this new trilateral relationship, and openly explore whether trilateral dialogue will make sense and be feasible. The three authors of the background papers were asked to address these questions as the basis for discussion at the Beijing workshop. Initiation of the trilateral dialogue process in Beijing was predicated, however, on some fundamental premises also addressed by the authors.

The first premise was that trilateral cooperation would benefit not only the three partners but also the entire Asia Pacific region. China, whose largest trade partners are the United States and Japan, would benefit from a formal economic partnership to strengthen and expand the trilateral ties of economic interdependence. Likewise, the United States and Japan could foster greater regional security and prosperity through encouraging fuller participation by China in the multilateral international system. Conversely, friction among the three large economic powers could seriously undermine regional stability and prosperity. Trilateral cooperation among the three major powers in Asia should not be seen by other countries in the region as a joint conspiracy, but rather as efforts to share their responsibilities.

Second, building a harmonious relationship poses a major challenge for the three partners. Clearly there is no auspicious historical precedent for cooperation among the three countries. Equitable relations among them will be extremely difficult to achieve, as each party tends to envision a nightmarish scenario of the two other nations ganging up on it. A traditional concern in Japan is that the United States may revive its strong affinity for China and form a new China-U.S. relationship, bypassing Japan. Some Americans worry that the two Asian powers may forge a "China-Japan condominium" that might serve as the cornerstone of an East Asian bloc. Similarly, the Chinese are anxious about possible U.S.-Japan collaboration to "contain" China. As a matter of fact, each of the three bilateral relationships had deteriorated in the months preceding the Beijing workshop, and this had tended to reinforce each country's suspicions or concerns about the intentions of the other two. The U.S.-Japan Joint Declaration on Security Cooperation, which was signed in April 1996, a month after the missile firing in the Taiwan Strait, is one example of several international developments that had aroused tensions.

A third premise was that the trilateral relationship should be based on solid bilateral relationships, but, at the same time, the trilateral relationship should help strengthen such bilateral relationships. It was recognized that building a constructive Sino-Japanese relationship is a special challenge, as interactions between China and Japan have been troubled by several difficult factors, and these factors could undermine harmonious trilateral relations. In particular, history and nationalism are major constraints against a better bilateral relationship, and these factors may be even more exacerbated in the coming years. Sentiment is growing in Japan that China is using the "history card" to prevent Japan from becoming a superpower, though there are many Japanese who feel the need for Japan to come to terms with its own history as a prerequisite to a constructive relationship with China. There are also several significant unresolved bilateral issues, including the territorial issue of the Senkaku/Diaoyu Islands. The Sino-Japanese relationship is further complicated by the fact that China is a nuclear power with the potential to become a global economic power, whereas Japan, which presently provides economic assistance vital to China's economic development, is committed to maintaining its status as a nonmilitary, civilian power.

Fourth, mutual perceptions diverge and shift considerably over time, thus complicating management of the trilateral relationship. This is perhaps most pronounced in the U.S. view of China. There is a tendency on the part of some Americans in recent years to "demonize" China, but during the 1970s and 1980s, when cold war tensions were high, the Soviet Union, not China, was the major concern of the United States. A more positive atmosphere prevailed in the China-U.S. relationship in the post–Gang of Four era when reforms took place in China. Full diplomatic relations were established between Beijing and Washington in 1979. The Tiananmen Square incident in 1989 again changed things quite drastically, politicizing U.S. policies toward China. Such shifting perceptions within the bilateral relationship will make the management of the trilateral relationship even more complicated.

Fifth and related to the above, management of the trilateral relationship has become more complicated by the growing tendency of domestic sociopolitical dynamics to intrude on the foreign policy of each nation, which reflects the power of globalization and the greater interdependence among nations. In other words, there are more actors in the formulation and implementation of each nation's foreign policies. Each nation's leadership feels a greater need to have broad-based support for its foreign policy direction, and the traditional foreign policy designed by a small number of "the best and the brightest" cannot operate at its own discretion anymore.

The sixth premise was that despite many challenges and constraints, it can be assumed that there is a strong interest in the three countries in managing the trilateral relationship. There is a general understanding in Japan and the United States on the need to come to grips with an increasingly powerful China, regardless of emotional attachments or reservations about China. China, too, recognizes that it must learn to manage the multilateral relationship, a skill many Chinese leaders admit is not their forte.

THE ROLE OF DIALOGUE
IN MANAGING THE TRILATERAL RELATIONSHIP

The China-Japan-U.S. Research and Dialogue Project was initiated with a strong belief on the part of the organizers that promoting private-level dialogue among the three countries will be essential in managing the complex trilateral relationship. "Dialogues," or other related activities such as joint research, conferences, symposia, and information exchanges that may come under the rubric of "intellectual exchange," have played a positive role in the development of relations between nations and regions over the years. The Bilderberg Conferences played a critical role in the reconstruction of the Atlantic relationship after World War II. The Shimoda Conference series, which was started in 1967 as a forum of nongovernmental policy dialogue between Japan and the United States involving opinion leaders from diverse professional backgrounds, has set a pattern of broad and substantive communications between the two countries. The Trilateral Commission, which was established in 1973 bringing together leading private citizens of the advanced industrial democracies of Japan, North America, and Europe, has promoted closer cooperation among the three regions in addressing international economic and politico-security issues. In recent years, track two activities, or private-sector intellectual exchange and dialogues, have proliferated in Asia Pacific, and joint efforts by private policy research institutions, such as the Council for Security Cooperation in Asia Pacific (CSCAP), have been regarded as a critical element in building an Asia Pacific regional community. It was felt that the management of the China-Japan-U.S. trilateral relationship should take advantage of several useful functions of existing nongovernmental dialogue efforts.

Perhaps the most critical contribution that the trilateral dialogue among China, Japan, and the United States can make is to reorient the mindset of policymakers and policy thinkers of these countries, which share a "cultural arrogance," as Funabashi expresses it, to the new reality of the world. Abramowitz points out that "although the three countries are not oblivious to the power relationships between them, they do not think in trilateral terms." Wang compares the China-Japan-U.S. trilateral relationship with the previous China-Soviet-U.S. triangular relationship and contends that "the two trilateral relationships have shared one feature: two parties talk on a bilateral basis about the third party, and trilateral discussions are rarely held." Funabashi maintains that "the three countries are not accustomed to thinking trilaterally." In the work of the Trilateral Commission of Japan, North America, and Europe, this writer, having been involved in the exercise from its inception as the Japanese director, considers the most beneficial impact of the "trilateral process" to have been to force its members to consider policy issues in a multilateral context and encourage adjustments in the actions and behaviors of their countries accordingly. The nature of such adjustments was typically described by one of the members as discouraging the United States from "unilateral action" and Japan from "unilateral inaction."

The trilateral dialogue will encourage sharing of the same information and enhance knowledge about each other, reducing misperceptions and stereotyping. Such information and knowledge sharing is particularly important in enhancing the trilateral relationship between China, Japan, and the United States, which have distinctly different historical and cultural backgrounds, and, as noted before, among which concerns and suspicions about each other's intentions abound, particularly about the possibility of two of the three ganging up on the third. Particular emphasis should be given to the understanding of changing sociopolitical and economic dynamics reflecting increasing domestic diversity and pluralism in all three countries.

One function of the dialogue is to build a close working relationship among the partners. Zbigniew Brezezinski, who was director of the Trilateral Commission, used to point to the importance of "developing the habit of working together" through the work and dialogue of the Commission. In more conventional parlance, this may be called a confidence-building process. The habit of working together makes it possible for the participants in the dialogue to have shared understanding of the issues confronting them and think together about the joint responses. It is believed that this "sharing process" will eventually lead to the sharing of values, which is critical in building a sense of community among the parties.

Private-level dialogue can be a trailblazer and an agenda setter. As the discussion of possible establishment of official trilateral consultations among China, Japan, and the United States underscores, it is often difficult to start a new and innovative mechanism in the relationships among countries. There have been instances where private-level track two diplomacy paved the way for more official consultative mechanisms. CSCAP, a nongovernmental forum founded under the auspices of the ASEAN Institutes of Strategic and International Studies (ASEAN-ISIS), is considered to have inspired the governments concerned to create the ASEAN Regional Forum (ARF), which conducts governmental consultations on a new framework for Asia Pacific regional security. Though it is not certain whether there was a direct causal relationship, the Trilateral Commission did set the stage for the creation of the economic summit that met for the first time at Rambouillet in 1975. Similarly, nongovernmental dialogue forums can play the role of agenda setter for official dialogues and consultations. CSCAP plays this role for the official ARF, and the Eminent Persons Group (EPG) under the leadership of Fred Bergsten, director of the Institute of International Economy, has acted as agenda setter for the meetings of the Asia Pacific Economic Cooperation (APEC) forum.

Private dialogue forums can also involve leaders of diverse sectors in each society in policy-oriented discussions. As noted earlier, given the present phenomenon of globalization and pluralization of each society, participation of private leaders from various fields of activities is becoming essential in managing external relations. As a corollary to this point, these dialogue forums with other countries can in turn generate domestic debate on foreign policy issues. It should be recognized also that these dialogue forums can assume a "public education" function.

Though we must be careful not to become overly ambitious about what one project can accomplish, there is nevertheless a need to have a clearer idea as to the role and functions of China-Japan-U.S. trilateral dialogue. The Beijing workshop and the essays presented here did suggest that there clearly is a role to be played by such private-level dialogue. There also was a clear consensus at the Beijing workshop that trilateral dialogue is possible. As Wang writes, there was a strong recognition that "only through candid and substantive three-way exchanges of views can a constructive trilateral relationship between China, Japan, and the United States be established."

THE WAY FORWARD: MAKE HASTE SLOWLY

The three chapters of this book discuss not only the feasibility of the trilateral relationship between China, Japan, and the United States but also the possible agenda and procedures for dialogue activities. The Beijing workshop also addressed these issues in a very positive and constructive manner. The organizers of future trilateral dialogue should be mindful of several elements that were part of the deliberations in the trilateral joint exploration thus far.

First, it is important to emphasize the nongovernmental nature of the dialogue. One comparative advantage of track two diplomacy is that the dialogues can take place with a longer-term perspective and a broader definition of the respective national interests. Private dialogue can allow the participants to be candid in presenting their views, uninhibited by the diverse constraints that government officials face. This allows intellectual integrity for the participants and forthright intellectual engagements. Governments could be tempted to "manage" the track two diplomacy, but such an approach would be contradictory in nature and most probably counterproductive.

Second, the dialogue's agenda should be set carefully after substantive preparation. It is important to make sure that the agenda will integrally engage all three parties. Another consideration is to make use of the comparative advantage of the private nature of the dialogue. Abramowitz suggests that "this trialogue could be used as a way of discussing and perhaps helping diminish long-standing historical and psychological grievances among all the parties." In a similar vein, Wang suggests that trilateral discussion on topics that are "divisive and may involve political sensitivities both internationally and domestically," such as Chinese concerns over the U.S.-Japan security relationship, "may be more fruitful and sustainable when initially conducted on an unofficial basis."

Third, an important element to enhance the trilateral dialogue is to promote the overlappings of the three parties. What the three essays contained in this volume and the dialogue at the Beijing workshop confirmed is that the shared interests of the three countries are indeed quite extensive. The three countries clearly have a common stake in the future development and stability of Asia Pacific. The Korean peninsula is another area of possible trilateral cooperation as the three parties have a shared interest in its peaceful evolution.

Fourth, as mentioned earlier, the three partners should be sensitive to the possible concerns of other Asian nations about the nature of dialogue between the three major powers of the region. The management of the trilateral relationship is of vital interest to all the nations in the Asia Pacific region, and it is important to keep the trilateral discussion transparent to others and to involve, at times, participants from other countries to provide their perspective on the China-Japan-U.S. relationship, particularly the implications of that relationship on them.

Lastly, it should be remembered that such dialogue on the private level has to be carried out with a long-term impact in mind. Although it is clear from the preceding discussion that it is of urgent and critical importance for the three major powers in Asia Pacific to start the trilateral dialogue among themselves, developing such dialogue requires building mutual confidence, friendship, and the habit of working together. This is, by nature, a time-consuming and evolutionary process. With this in mind, the organizers of the Research and Dialogue Project have started a joint research project involving emerging intellectual leaders of the three countries. A study group of young Japanese scholars and researchers has been working almost a year and has produced a set of monographs on the China-Japan-U.S. relationship. They already made a dialogue trip to Beijing and Shanghai. Similarly, a study group of young Chinese intellectuals has been organized and has already made a dialogue trip to Japan. A similar study group is being planned in the United States. It is hoped that the three study groups will eventually meet together for an intense and future-oriented dialogue. Meanwhile, the senior group of intellectual leaders including the three authors of this book and others from the three countries will continue the dialogue that was started in Beijing in December 1996.

Indeed, the organizers of the China-Japan-U.S. Research and Dialogue Project have a contradictory sense of timing. The trialogue has to move forward rapidly and without delay, but it also has to be pursued in an evolutionary and perhaps time-consuming manner. This writer reminds himself that after the Trilateral Commission was created in 1973, the Japanese group was not willing to discuss security issues in the first six or seven years for fear of being criticized for promoting a collective security arrangement that is considered to be unconstitutional in Japan. When private dialogue between the United States and Japan was started at the Shimoda Conference in 1967, the conference site was visited by several hundred demonstrators. It took several years before the Socialist leaders became full-fledged participants in such dialogues.

In conceiving the project, Funabashi Yoichi and this writer set the target of ten years as the time frame when the three countries may be ready to organize a nongovernmental dialogue forum similar to the Trilateral Commission or the Shimoda Conference with the participation of leading private citizens from politics, business, academia, the media, nongovernmental organizations, and other fields. Nevertheless, this does not give those who believe in the critical importance of the trilateral dialogue all that much time for preparation. We have to move fast. It is hoped that this small volume of essays will offer a basic framework and a future agenda for such efforts.

In conclusion, the organizers of this project wish to express their sincere gratitude, first, to the Nippon Foundation for its generous financial support and encouragement, and to other funders, including the Ford Foundation and the Asia Pacific Agenda Project, which is a consortium of research institutions in Asia Pacific that jointly manage funds provided by the Japanese government.

CHINA-JAPAN-U.S.

Building a Constructive Relationship

Wang Jisi

SINCE THE END OF THE COLD WAR, the trilateral (*sanbian* in Chinese) or triangular (*sanjiao*) relationship among China, Japan, and the United States has been an increasingly popular topic in China's policy-oriented research circles. Analysts are giving more thought to the significance of China-Japan-U.S. interaction, the present structure of this three-way relationship, and different images of the United States and Japan in China that may influence China's respective policies toward them. It is vital that the important issues scholars and policy analysts of the three nations may conduct research on, and make proposals about, be identified so that improvement of the trilateral relationship will serve their respective national interests and the common good of the whole world.

DEFINING THE ISSUE

Three factors are contributing to this interest in China-Japan-U.S. relations. First, the Chinese approach to analyzing international politics remains state-centered. Chinese perceptions of the international structure (*geju*) based on changing relations and balance of forces among great powers provide the rationale for China's foreign policy orientation and readjustment.

In recent years, the most frequently used concept in the Chinese press is perhaps "multipolarization" (*duojihua*), which is described as both a desirable end and an inevitable trend. According to China's official line, the world will be safer, more peaceful, and enjoy more justice if the greatest pole—the United States—is less weighty and dominant in international affairs. Meanwhile, many poles, including China, Russia, Japan, the European Union, and some other regional states and groupings, are rising up, gaining more weight, or becoming more assertive in international affairs. The consensus among China's political analysts is that the international structure is actually moving toward this end.

Since the mid-1980s, it has been a standard observation in China that America is a declining power, whereas both China and Japan are playing a more important role in regional and global affairs. Therefore, it is essential for China to reassess the power relations of the three poles in order to define the trend toward multipolarization. Japan is seen as becoming more assertive in dealing with the United States in economic affairs and less dependent on U.S. advice on international issues. If the three powers are indeed "more equal" than ever before, it should be meaningful to deliberate the trilateral relationship.

Noting the recovery and good performance of the American economy in the mid-1990s, some Chinese observers now argue that the United States is gaining the upper hand in economic competition with Japan and Europe. The United States, according to these observers, is no less influential in global and regional affairs than several years ago, and will remain the only truly global power in the foreseeable future. Their conclusion is that multipolarity is not yet the reality, and therefore the international structure is "one superpower, many great powers" (yichaoduoqiang). Some analysts even contend that the situation today is that the superpower is more super, and the many great powers are less great. Despite the ramifications of opinion among Chinese political analysts about the current international structure, the relative power of the United States vis-à-vis Japan and China provides the rationale for China's foreign policy orientation and adjustment.

A second reason for the renewed focus on trilateral relations is that Japan and the United States continue to be China's No. 1 and No. 2 trading partners in spite of China's largely successful effort in recent years to diversify its foreign economic relations. They are also the largest foreign (Hong Kong and Taiwan are not considered "foreign") investors in China. Japan-U.S. trade relations and economic competition, especially within the framework of the Asia Pacific Economic Cooperation (APEC) forum, have important implications for China's economic growth.

Third, with Russia's role diminished in East Asian regional affairs, there is now less interest in examining the China-Japan-U.S.-Russia "quadrangle," which was an appealing notion some years ago. The Association of Southeast Asian Nations is more vocal in setting the regional agenda, but its relevance to Northeast Asian security is limited. Both North Korea and South Korea are preoccupied with their bilateral tensions. No other powers are likely to match the "big three" in shaping the regional order in Asia Pacific.

The growing Chinese interest in addressing the China-Japan-U.S. trilaterality is reinforced by comparable discussions in Japan and, to a lesser degree, in the United States. There have already been numerous symposia in the past two to three years among Chinese, Japanese, and American scholars on the trilateral relationship.

It is only natural that Americans are less galvanized than their Chinese and Japanese counterparts to focus on this subject. Although Japan is America's second largest trading partner (next to Canada), China ranks only fifth in America's foreign trade. Besides, Europe weighs at least as heavily as Asia in America's strategic thinking. In comparison, America is Japan's largest trading partner, and China is next only to America. No other countries are as weighty as America or China in Japan's international outlook and security considerations. As mentioned earlier, relations with Japan and the United States are always at the top of the agenda in China's foreign affairs. Different orders of priority in foreign relations cause an asymmetry of attention to the tripartite relationship in the three countries.

The China-Japan-U.S. tripartite relationship is different in some fundamental ways from the so-called China-Soviet-U.S. triangle in the 1970s–1980s and the tripartite Western alliance of the United States, Western Europe, and Japan. In the China-Soviet-U.S. triangle, the United States viewed the Soviet Union as its major strategic and ideological opponent in the world arena, and the Soviet Union felt the same way about the United States. A less powerful player, China was nonetheless in a position to tilt the balance between the two superpowers by moving closer to either. Their three-way interaction and maneuvering were motivated mainly by security concerns, and economic factors were not of considerable importance. The tripod of the Western alliance was also directed against Soviet expansion in the cold war years, but this club of developed countries has proven to be durable even after the demise of the Soviet Union due to their common economic interests and shared political values. There are certainly economic frictions, competitions, and divergence of strategic interests between the United States, the European powers, and Japan, but none of their bilateral relationships harbors the extent of tensions evident today between China and the United States.

It is sensible and justifiable to study China-Japan-U.S. relations from a trilateral perspective, as each bilateral connection within the three influences, and is influenced by, the third party's behavior. Here are some aspects and examples:

- Although both Tokyo and Washington insist that their security alliance is not directed at China, it would be unwise to deny that the rising power of China and the country's perceived assertiveness is a major backdrop to their sustained security relations.
- Chinese leaders have recently reiterated their concerns about unfavorable implications of U.S.-Japan military ties. In particular, Chinese analysts fear that China's deterrence against Taiwan independence may be countered by U.S.-Japan cooperation.
- In U.S.-Chinese dialogues, American strategic thinkers do not squarely discredit the Chinese worry that Japan's political ambitions backed by increasing military capabilities might lead to instability in the Asia Pacific region. Instead, they have tried to convince their Chinese counterparts that close U.S.-Japan ties can serve the purpose of restraining any possible excessive ambitions and irresponsible behavior of Japan.
- U.S. officials and analysts point to the potential rivalry between Japan and China, among other reasons, to justify continued American military presence in the Western Pacific. Washington has delicately indicated neutrality toward the territorial dispute between China and Japan over the Diaoyu Islands (the Senkaku Islands to the Japanese).

- Japanese officials express their anxiety about the Sino-American relationship whenever it goes awry. On the other hand, if Beijing and Washington seem to be on good terms with each other, the Japanese are likely to make the point that improvement of their bilateral relations should not be achieved at Japan's expense. Japan's sensitivity to the amelioration in Sino-American relations since the latter part of 1996 is particularly evident.
- Chinese observers have taken note of the fact that Japan and the United States hold different views about China. Compared with the United States, Japan reacted more mildly to the political unrest in Beijing in 1989 and has been reluctant to join Americans' abrasive criticisms of China's human rights record. This Japanese attitude may have contributed to the moderation of Washington's China policy, especially in terms of its human rights discord with Beijing. Thus in Chinese eyes, Japan does not seem to pose a meaningful political threat. In contrast, the Chinese leadership vigorously calls for vigilance against American political, ideological, and cultural penetration into Chinese society.

If the previous China-Soviet-U.S. triangular relationship was highlighted by summit meetings, communiqués, public gestures, and military cooperation, often aimed at gaining bargaining power for immediate results, the present China-Japan-U.S. trilateral relationship is characterized by behind-the-scenes persuasions, informal exchanges of views, and quiet gestures that reflect long-term interests and calculations. But the two trilateral relationships have shared one feature: two parties talk on a bilateral basis about the third party, and trilateral discussions are rarely held. Only through candid and substantive three-way exchanges of views can a constructive trilateral relationship between China, Japan, and the United States be established.

DELINEATING THE STRUCTURE

A better understanding of the structure of China-Japan-U.S. relations must take into account the new realities of globalization.

Nine years have passed since the sea changes in Eastern Europe that shattered the bipolar structure of global politics. But political analysts all over the world are still unable to narrow their differences in characterizing post–cold war world politics. They may have to be as accustomed to this lack of common interpretation as statesmen are to dealing with the complexity and disorder of the real world itself.

In the United States, post–cold war visions have ranged from "the end of history" to the "clash of civilizations." In Japan, commentators seem to hold diversified views in identifying the features of world politics today. In China's political vocabulary, "multipolarization" and "one superpower, many great powers" are the more acceptable abstractions. However, no general agreement has yet been reached among Chinese observers as to how many "poles" or "great powers" there are and will be, how the power balance will evolve among them, and, more importantly, what will be the central conflicts in the future.

The lack of a common characterization of the international structure portends vacillation of the foreign policies of the great powers and volatility of their relationships. At the same time, people concerned about international stability increasingly have to look beyond nation-states and their power relations for sources of, and solutions to, transnational tensions. The issues previously described as those of "low politics," such as terrorism, illegal immigration, drug trafficking, and environmental pollution, are moving onto central agendas of and between national leaders. Nonetheless, traditional security problems related to territorial disputes, sovereignty, and arms control continue to loom large, particularly in East Asia. There is no imminent international war in this region, but the range and complexity of security problems, and possible intensity of some of them, allow no time for complacency.

Domestic problems in the United States, Japan, and China are making a strong impact on relationships among the three powers, and in turn would be exacerbated by international tensions in the Asia Pacific region. The ability of the United States to intervene in the affairs of other states is seriously hampered by the absence of a widely agreed organizing principal for its foreign policy. Economic interests, regional peace and stability, traditional security concerns like nuclear nonproliferation and arms control, and human rights considerations are vying for priority on the U.S. foreign policy agenda. More fundamentally, chronic domestic problems, such as ethnic tensions, social decay, immorality, distrust of government, and crime, are eroding the edifice of American society within and damaging its image without. In Japan, the end of one-party dominance in 1993 and the following successive multiparty governments have yet to reveal a political order that provides strong leadership, real reform, and enlarged international responsibilities. China has enjoyed a high rate of economic growth, but the central government is preoccupied with the domestic tasks of fighting rampant corruption and redressing economic discrepancies.

Of the bilateral relationships between Tokyo, Beijing, and Washington, Japan-U.S. ties are the closest. Despite the chronic economic friction and competition, Japan and the United States are after all security and political allies. There is a strong basis for the United States and Japan to coordinate their approaches to China that differ in degree and style but not in kind. U.S.-China ties are the most strained and unstable. As for the Japan-China connection, there seems to be no possibility that the two countries will form a strategic alliance that would make their relations closer than the ties between Japan and the United States. Nor is their bilateral relationship likely to become worse than that between China and the United States. In terms of overall wealth and technological prowess, the United States takes the lead, followed by Japan, and China is the weakest. Although both Chinese and Japanese often talk about their cultural affinity under "Asian civilization," in reality Japan and the United States have more common political values to share. These basic patterns of power relations will not go away in the foreseeable future.

The close strategic ties between Japan and the United States have helped reduce their economic conflict to a manageable level. But the problems leading to their trade frictions are tenacious and deep-rooted in their respective societies. The Americans strongly demand that Japan should shift decisively away from the alleged neomercantilist economic policies and business practices, yet they must be patient and persistent. They should also readjust their own economic policies and business practices at home.

While domestic political constraints in Japan are preventing major economic policy changes in response to U.S. pressures, market forces are pushing Japanese businesses to transfer production facilities to other East Asian countries, noticeably China. In international affairs, Japan has become much less reluctant to take positions different from the United States while strengthening relations with the rest of Asia. However, Japan's governmental and business leadership is well aware that Japan's major economic and security interests lie with the Western world.

Problems between China and the United States abound. Areas of difficulty range from human rights to intellectual property rights, from Taiwan to arms sales and nonproliferation. Each issue area has experienced a series of crises in the past few years. At the same time, bilateral trade and U.S. investment in China have been soaring. Educational, cultural, scientific, and technological exchanges continue to develop despite the political discord. Disney, Microsoft, and Coca-Cola have become part of the daily life of many urban Chinese.

Sino-Japanese economic cooperation is growing almost as rapidly as Sino-U.S. commercial relations. On the whole, the atmosphere of Sino-Japanese official relations in the last few years has been markedly better than that between Beijing and Washington. However, at both popular and elite levels in China, there is a fervent resentment against the effort made by some Japanese to deny imperial Japan's aggression and atrocities in Asia during World War II. On the Japanese side, people harbor ambivalent feelings about the rise of China. In addition, the territorial dispute over the Diaoyu Islands has recently brought to the fore another source of Sino-Japanese controversy.

In all these three relationships, this peculiar combination of contention and cooperation reflects the bewildering impact of globalization in the post–cold war era. No policy of one country toward another can be constructed on a single, unambiguous foundation. All policies are motivated and restrained by each country's respective domestic needs and social changes.

In this context, a series of questions is raised, particularly in China, regarding U.S.-Japan security relations in the post–cold war era. In China's judgment, the Asia Pacific region is enjoying an unprecedented peaceful and stable security environment despite a few potential flashpoints. But why is the Japan-U.S. Security Treaty deemed necessary by both Washington and Tokyo and has even been solidified by a new joint declaration in April 1996 and the guidelines that followed? Is, or to what extent is, the Security Treaty directed at China? Why is Washington seemingly encouraging Japan to play a larger role in Asian security affairs?

Some Japanese and Americans have tried to convince Chinese officials and strategists that their governments have sustained the security relationship by its own momentum in the absence of an identifiable threat rather than by rigorous strategic rationale. Others simply deny there is anything new or alarming. Still others argue that common concerns about North Korea are the main reason for renewing the security relationship. Some analysts emphasize the motives of Japan's ruling elite to consolidate its domestic position in signing the joint declaration. However, a few outspoken American and Japanese officials and commentators have admitted that the strengthening of security cooperation is designed to cope with the emerging "China problem," with the recent tensions in the Taiwan Strait as the major factor in redefining the Japan-U.S. military alliance.

Since not all these explanations can be true, further clarification of Japanese and American intentions is imperative. The Americans constantly call for "military transparency," and a variety of proposals have been put forward for establishing multilateral security mechanisms in the Asia Pacific region. If Tokyo and Washington want others to be more cooperative in Asian security affairs, they should show adequate transparency and candor in specifying their own concerns and plans. It is often stated that the United States and Japan share an interest in seeing China unified and effectively governed and integrated into the emerging Pacific community. Both words and deeds are needed to prove this interest.

The concept of "security dilemma" seems relevant to the maintenance of international security in East Asia today. A state is likely to be subject to this security dilemma: In its efforts to preserve or enhance its own security, this state can take measures, such as building arms and forming alliances, that decrease the security of other states and that cause them in turn to take countermeasures that neutralize the actions of this state and that may even menace it. Then this state may feel impelled to take additional actions that will provoke additional countermeasures . . . and so forth. Such an action-reaction spiral can occur between two states or among several of them, precipitating an arms race and heading for confrontation.

Compared with China, the United States and Japan are economically much stronger and their respective defense systems are more advanced. If their security alliance is aimed at deterring a rising China that is nonetheless still much weaker than them, China will certainly feel insecure—for good reason. The security dilemma will be further aggravated when many Chinese suspect that the United States and Japan are attempting to play the "Taiwan card," i.e., backing the pro-independence forces in Taiwan to threaten and humiliate China. The rising clamor in both Japan and the United States describing China as a strategic threat is just feeding these Chinese suspicions.

Military alliances, in the traditional sense of two powers allying against a third party, and simplistic rationale in identifying threats will not be helpful in seeking solutions to the increasingly complicated security problems in the Asia Pacific region, including those of low politics. The age of globalization and information calls for new confidence-building visions and measures that take into account the complex realities we are faced with today.

COMPARING THE IMAGES OF THE
UNITED STATES AND JAPAN IN CHINA

Since the collapse of the Soviet Union, the United States and Japan have been by far the most important two countries to China in political, economic, and security terms. Ironically, they are also the most frequently criticized countries in the Chinese press. To be sure, the Chinese media gives considerable positive coverage of both the United States and Japan, describing the advanced economic development, management, public administration, culture, education, science, technology, and civilization in each of the two societies. Here we will look at only the negative part of their public images in China.

In the political realm, both the United States and Japan are generally depicted as attempting to undermine China's socialist system. However, as mentioned earlier, the United States is seen by Beijing as much more vigorously pursuing the goal of making the life of the Chinese leadership more difficult. Chinese leaders now openly attack the United States for maintaining a policy designed to westernize China and split China up. In contrast, although Japan is one of the "Western powers" as measured by its stage of economic development, it is also sometimes identified as belonging to the Asian nations that collectively as well as individually resist the Americans' pressure to impose their political will on Asia. Furthermore, according to many Chinese commentators, American demands that Asian countries should follow the U.S. political model and human rights criteria are resulting in an intense cultural conflict between the United States and East Asia. Japan, on the other hand, with its perceived cultural affinity with China and other Asian nations, may eventually embark on a political ship not steered by the United States.

In terms of international economics, Japan also enjoys a favorable image in China. The Chinese press often reports U.S.-Japan trade friction in a manner sympathetic to the Japanese. American negotiators are described as unreasonably arrogant and easily resorting to high-handed sanctions. American calls for speeding up the pace and enlarging the scope of the liberalization of trade and investment in the Asia Pacific region lead to the Chinese concern that the United States may try to take advantage of its economic power to achieve political goals unacceptable to China. The long-term effect of regional liberalization may be conducive to China's economy, but the Chinese are not yet ready to welcome the American proposals in APEC on liberalization, which are posing great challenges to China's current foreign trade policies, industrial structure, and price system.

Beijing sees U.S. opposition as the greatest obstacle to its strenuous effort for membership in the World Trade Organization (WTO). Many Chinese commentators believe that the Americans' unwillingness to see the rise of China as a greater economic partner is the actual thinking in Washington behind its explanation that China's accession to the WTO is unacceptable at this stage only because of economic considerations. Meanwhile, Japan signed in 1997 a bilateral agreement with China supporting China's bid for WTO membership. This Japanese move will certainly be appreciated in Beijing.

China has declared its support for Malaysia's proposal for the formulation of the East Asia Economic Caucus (EAEC) that excludes the United States. In Chinese eyes, the key element preventing EAEC from being established is America's opposition, and Japan's attitude is circumspect due mainly to American pressure. China welcomes the general trend that trade, technological interflow, and investment among Asian countries are increasing measurably and thus reducing their reliance on American connections. Japan is the key accelerator of this trend.

Security is probably the only aspect in which China's attitude is somewhat ambiguous between Japan and the United States. To be sure, the newly enhanced Japan-U.S. security cooperation has unambiguously reinforced Chinese anxiety about these two powers' joint effort to counterweight Chinese power. A major question asked by Chinese analysts is, "Which one of the two should be held more responsible for this joint effort?" While some of the Chinese criticisms of the Japan-U.S. alliance stress Japan's motivations to strengthen its independent military capabilities, the major Chinese target is still the United States. After all, it is the United States that is the stronger of the two military machines and thus poses the greater challenge to China's national defense and to the task of Chinese national reunification.

On balance, the image of the United States compares unfavorably with that of Japan in China. This conclusion can be reinforced by reading the political report by Chinese leader Jiang Zemin at the 15th National Congress of the Communist Party of China held in October 1997. The negative U.S. image results mainly from constant U.S. pressure on China regarding human rights issues, China's resistance to Western political ideas, and Sino-American tensions regarding the Taiwan problem. However, the recent souring of Sino-Japanese relations gives little reason for Japan to be complacent. Chinese publications have indicated a strong public aversion to the unrepentant attitude of some Japanese toward Japan's wrongdoing during World War II. The Japanese statements that the scope of Japan-U.S. defense cooperation should include the Taiwan area have triggered Chinese repugnance and alert. If Japan continues to appear insensitive to Chinese feelings and interests, Beijing might someday seek a more balanced position between Tokyo and Washington.

IDENTIFYING TRILATERAL TOPICS

Since some trilateral issues among China, Japan, and the United States, such as Chinese concerns over the Japan-U.S. security relationship, can be very divisive and may involve political sensitivities both internationally and domestically, discussion of them in trilateral settings may be more fruitful and sustainable when initially conducted on an unofficial basis. The following are some possible questions of interest.

The perceived "rise of China." One central question in discussing the trilateral relationship is how to assess the rising power of China, which is the major force in changing the geopolitical and geoeconomic realities in the Asia Pacific region. In the United States and Japan, there are conflicting assessments and projections of China's political stability and economic development. Many Chinese are proud of China's achievements and are fond of talking about the twenty-first century as an "Asian century" or "Chinese century," but they are perplexed by the fear in the outside world of China's growth. Some other Chinese, noting the serious discrepancies and difficulties in the path of China's development, caution against exaggerations of China's potential. They view unrealistic estimations of China's growth as tending to mislead Japanese and American policies toward China.

Security issues. The major stumbling block to establishing a cooperative—and probably more equilateral—relationship between the three nations seems to be the perception that China is viewed by Americans and Japanese as a potential threat and therefore is becoming the main target of the Japan-U.S. security alliance. A defensive Chinese reaction to the "China threat" notion should be taken for granted. It will be useful for the Japanese and American sides to articulate their respective views and common concerns about the rise of China. A somewhat theoretical but crucial question is whether a security alliance should be maintained without any designated enemy country.

Chinese commentators find it legitimate to remind Japan of its wrongdoings in China and other parts of Asia during World War II with the fear that Japanese denial of war crimes forebodes the revival of militarism. The Japanese response to these worries seems rather obscure and contradictory. A wartime ally with China against Japan, America's attitude toward this Sino-Japanese dispute appears to be one of indifference. A candid three-way discussion should pave the way for deeper understanding.

America's role in Asian security is another area of interest that deserves sufficient attention. Despite recurrent doubts in the United States and Japan about Washington's long-term willingness to maintain the American military presence in Northeast Asia due to neo-isolationism at home, few, if any, Chinese analysts believe that U.S. forces would withdraw voluntarily. In fact, many of them hold deep suspicions that U.S. defense industries are a strong factor supporting the continued presence of American bases in the region, and that China is deliberately depicted by the Americans as a destabilizing power in order to justify U.S. military spending. Japanese comments on these Chinese feelings should be welcomed.

Economic issues. As Morton Abramowitz points out, "probably the easiest subjects on which to initiate fruitful trilateral discussion are economic and environmental cooperation activities." These subjects may include:

- a comparison of U.S. trade deficits with China and Japan
- implications of U.S.-Japan trade frictions for China
- implications of U.S.-China trade negotiations as well as agreements on such issues as intellectual property rights for Japanese commercial relations with China
- China's economic reform and its impact on Japanese and American business interests in China
- economic competition and cooperation between America and Japan in China

- coordinating U.S., Japanese, and Chinese policies toward APEC and other global and regional organizations and regimes, including the Malaysian proposal to establish the EAEC
- Japanese and American positions on China's accession to the WTO
- contrasting developmental models and economic policies of Japan and the United States and what China can learn from them
- "Greater China," i.e., Chinese mainland-Taiwan-Hong Kong connections and their implications for U.S. and Japanese business opportunities
- possibilities of three-way cooperation on environmental issues.

"Asian values" and domestic changes. Academic deliberations of such subjects as the "clash of civilizations" may well reflect political thinking as well as some political realities. "The Asianization of Japan" or otherwise (the Westernization of Japan?) would be stimulating, at least to the Chinese. China's political education of patriotism and socialist spiritual civilization will have bearings on foreign relations. As most parts of China and Japan are homogeneous in terms of ethnicity and culture, it will be interesting for Chinese and Japanese scholars to compare their comprehension of the ethnic/cultural diversity of the United States.

Regional dimensions. The Clinton administration has proposed the establishment of a "Pacific Community." Richard Solomon explains the notion by suggesting that "the most promising future one can anticipate for the coming period in East Asia is that of a loose balance of power among the states of the (U.S.-China-Japan-Russia) Strategic Quadrangle embodying areas of political and economic cooperation—with the U.S.-Japan alliance as the stabilizing core of the region."* Chinese publications have shown strong reservations about the concept of the Pacific Community if it is meant to exert America's "leadership role." What is Japan's response?

What Solomon refers to as "wild cards" in the Asia Pacific

*Michael Mandelbaum, ed., *Strategic Quadrangle: Russia, China, Japan, and the United States in East Asia*, New York: Council on Foreign Relations Press, 1995, p. 205.

region (tensions on the Korean peninsula, restless subnational forces, intraregional trade patterns tending to block broader economic integration, and so on)* are of course relevant to the China-Japan-U.S. trilateral relationship. They should be properly treated when trilateral interaction becomes constructive and regular.

*Ibid., pp. 206–207.

The Not-So-Plain Geometry of a Trilateral Relationship

Morton I. Abramowitz

THIS CHAPTER examines the dynamics of China-Japan-U.S. relations and identifies special factors that could contribute to the evolution of a constructive, three-way interaction among the countries that goes beyond their separate bilateral relationships. It will also provide a broad view of how the United States perceives its relations with China and Japan. It then will discuss an American sense of how China and Japan see their relations with each other and the United States and how each might view a trilateral relationship. Finally, the chapter will consider whether there is a good basis for either official or private three-way discussions among the three countries.

A NEW GEOMETRY?

The current intellectual thrashing about on the concept of a "new" trilateral relationship is of course a result of trying to come to grips with the vast economic and political changes in Asia in the last twenty years, particularly China's rapid economic development and the demise of the Soviet Union. The search is for measures that will increase stability among all the parties. To identify and implement such measures, the parties must look at relationships somewhat differently from the past—not an easy task.

The cold war geometry between China, the Soviet Union, and

the United States (with Japan as junior partner), has disappeared. Interrelationships are no longer axiomatic. Today, global economic forces, not geostrategy, seem to be driving political forces in the region. These forces, which are often beyond the control of governments, are pulling China, Japan, and the United States together in unprecedented ways, forging new links that are more and more costly to break. The United States is Japan's largest trading partner, and the United States and Japan are China's first and second largest trading partners. Thirty years ago, there was barely any trade with China.

There are major capital flows among the three countries. Japan, for example, is the largest foreign purchaser of U.S. government debt, and China recently emerged as a large purchaser. Both U.S. and Japanese firms are major direct investors in China, and they have been particularly important in supplying advanced technology in manufacturing. Economics and the new speed of global communications are changing domestic politics in all three countries. It is unclear what the results of all these changes will be, but the conventional wisdom seems to be that the future of East Asia will be largely determined by the three countries.

Thus, some feel the "trilateral relationship" is a new imperative, though no one has actually defined it. Is it to be a tripartite relationship, which connotes a positive entente of three? Or a triangular relationship, which implies a group of three parties maneuvering for advantage, in this case, the Japan-U.S. side maneuvering vis-à-vis China and vice versa? Or a true trilateral relationship, which suggests significant, unforeseen, three-way interaction, not necessarily always positive.

Even the word "trilateral" is a bit misleading. It suggests an equilateral triangle, but there is an asymmetrical distribution of power among China, Japan, and the United States that invariably raises suspicions. The two most developed, the United States and Japan, are treaty allies with capable forces, economic dynamism, and stable domestic systems. China is still mostly potential. For all its size, population, and international ethnic ties, China is behind economically, militarily, and scientifically and has a long way to go before it becomes a confident global political player. Many outsiders question China's stability and long-term intentions.

However, China's economic capabilities are growing, and, despite its weaknesses, its nuclear and missile forces loom large and potentially menacing, particularly to the Japanese defense community. Nevertheless, the great asymmetries of power that remain make it conceptually difficult to deal with a trilateral relationship.

Also, the term "trilateral" implies a multilateral dimension to relations among the three. But no multilateral institution exists in Northeast Asia, and there is no multilateral dimension to the interrelationships among the three, although institutionalized multilateralism is nascent in the economic field through the Asia Pacific Economic Cooperation (APEC) forum, to which all three belong. The Korean Peninsula Energy Development Organization (KEDO) is the closest thing that exists in Northeast Asia to an attempt to deal with certain security issues on a multilateral basis, but that is a long way from multilateralism in security matters.

For all three countries to participate in a trilateral relationship, each would have to perceive that they have a mutuality of at least some important interests in working together that outweighs negatives associated with doing so. Korea would seem to be an obvious case. But the great disparities of power, vastly different political systems, and long-established alignments remain central. At present, although the three countries are not oblivious to the power relationships between themselves, they do not think in trilateral terms. It will be difficult to move beyond the present state of things.

There is another obvious question: Why, in looking at the future of Northeast Asia, would we limit the major players to three? South Korea is a major player now—certainly in Northeast Asia— and will be even more so in the longer term. So will Russia in the long term, whatever its short-term infirmities.

AMERICAN PERCEPTIONS

American policymakers and outside specialists are divided on what a trilateral relationship would mean. Some believe that because of the importance of the three countries and the possibility of clashing interests, genuine tripartite collaboration has to be developed. Others dismiss this notion, saying there are, and for the foreseeable future can only be, in any practical sense, bilateral relations among the three, with a cautious eye cocked toward China. All agree that it is hard to find a triangular situation comparable to that of China, the Soviet Union, and the United States in the seventies and eighties, where the parties looked at bilateral actions in great part in terms of their impact on the third. The weakest party in that case was allied to the strongest, opposite to what we have now, where the two strongest are allied, but not necessarily against the third.

The biggest uncertainty and concern in the United States is China. There is confusion and contentious debate in the United States about China and the troubled state of U.S.-China relations, particularly between the legislative and executive branches. For five years or so, the executive branch effectively lost control of China policy. Now there is a growing consensus that China is the central foreign policy challenge for America in Asia, while U.S.-Japan relations are stable despite continuing trade disputes. The consensus stops there, however. The biggest concerns Americans have with China remain the nature of the Chinese government and how China will use its growing power, both economic and military, in the future.

China is a significant domestic political issue complicating any American administration's ability to manage policy. There are several different political constituencies on China: nostalgics, business, the human rights community, real-politikers. Competition between the constituencies has complicated the domestic politics of China policy and often focuses attention on single issues. Now both Left and Right seem to be intent on making China "Public Enemy No. 1."

Many Americans fear that China is rapidly becoming the next Japan, an economic superpower that runs large bilateral trade surpluses with the United States while protecting its own markets by a variety of indirect means. The U.S. trade deficit with China edged ahead of the deficit with Japan for the first time in June 1996. This recurred in August by a much wider margin, almost US$1 billion. The apprehension that China is following the Japanese economic model is reinforced by the emergence in China of industrial policies in key sectors. Thus, trade tensions have continued to grow, illustrating the double-edged nature of economic forces. Even as they pull the three countries toward each other, they create new sources of tension. Over time, a vast increase in China trade and investment will likely produce a strong domestic China lobby, which could affect U.S. dealings with Japan.

Though some Americans question its durability, the unequal Japan-U.S. alliance is still generally seen as the linchpin of deterrence and psychological security in Northeast Asia, although its impact goes well beyond China and North Korea. That a trilateral focus could politically weaken a critical strategic partnership between Washington and Tokyo with few compensating benefits would not be much of an American concern; but it might disquiet the Southeast Asians.

Americans nevertheless generally believe that the three countries, despite the varying tensions among them, can all have decent relationships with each other. Uneasy as they are about China, Americans generally view the present Asian situation as stable, although they fear that China will disturb that stability. Americans have an implicit security relationship with Taiwan, which they realize can cause difficulties with China. Most Americans do not now think in terms of one country playing off another, although events could change that. There are strong sentiments that American policy must contain a hedge against China becoming aggressive.

In the past, U.S. and Japanese views of China often diverged, particularly over whether to link trade and politics. This caused strains in otherwise close bilateral relations during the cold war. U.S. policy is much more susceptible to political shifts. Japan has never isolated itself from dealings with China, while the United States has periodically done so. The United States believes that Japan fears that U.S. mismanagement of dealings with China could leave Tokyo caught in the middle, yet Tokyo also fears being left to deal with China alone. U.S.-Japan differences on China, however, have never been allowed to get out of hand, and both countries are mindful of that possibility. Many American experts believe that the United States and Japan need to better sort out their views on China and coordinate their approach.

The U.S.-Japan alliance may of course be seen as anti-Chinese, and some in the United States want to make it so. Nevertheless, neither the United States nor Japan presently want to participate openly in a "contain China" policy. That is politically impossible in Tokyo and probably also the case at this point in the United States, although anti-China sentiment has grown in both countries as a result of Beijing's saber-rattling in the Taiwan Strait and human rights issues and, for Japan, the fracas over the Senkaku Islands (called the Diaoyu Islands by the Chinese).

AN AMERICAN ASSESSMENT OF JAPANESE PERCEPTIONS

Japanese foreign policy remains basically centered on the alliance with the United States, which serves Japanese security purposes in the region and continues to permit Japan to focus on economic and social issues. While there are always abrasions in the U.S.-Japan relationship, there are no serious efforts to get rid of or alter the alliance. That could change over time, although it is unlikely. Japan would like to supplement the alliance with a more satisfactory relationship with China, but for Japan there is presently no trade-off, nor any indication of Tokyo wanting to use its dealings with China to affect aspects of U.S.-Japan relations. Japan certainly does not want to be squeezed in acrimony between Washington and Beijing and therefore wants the United States to manage its relations with China in such a way as to minimize bilateral tensions. Among some Japanese there is a concern that the United States will eventually draw close to China and the hope that the United States will balance off growing Chinese power, or protect Japan against it.

While recognizing that China has reached a new eminence and is a power to be reckoned with, the Japanese remain ambivalent about China. Public sentiments toward China have waxed and waned. The present, growing distrust appears to have led to greater willingness to confront China directly, such as over the Senkakus, the only issue of direct contention between the two. That may not last long. Japanese are well aware of Japan's deep involvement in Hong Kong and in China's economy and do not want to endanger their relationship with China. History is still an important neuralgic factor in Chinese-Japanese relations, which encourages caution in Tokyo. On the other hand, Japan also has a special relationship with Taiwan and hopes the United States will sustain Taiwan's current autonomous status.

The Japanese are perhaps the most interested in a trilateral relationship; they seem to view a three-way discussion as part of a better multilateral engagement in Northeast Asia and another means of better incorporating China into the world. They see this approach as prudent in a changing climate, helpful educationally, and politically welcome at home.

The Japanese frequently reexamine their defense policies, particularly in light of possible changes in the Korean situation and the anticipated growth of China's military capabilities. Chinese (and potential Korean) missile capabilities are a concern of Japanese defense specialists. Missile defense may become a troublesome ingredient in both Japanese and Chinese relations and in the internal Chinese and Japanese political scenes. It is also an increasingly important issue with the United States that will need protracted discussion.

AN AMERICAN ASSESSMENT OF CHINESE PERCEPTIONS

China's opaqueness and government domination of the media and external discussion make it difficult for outsiders to feel comfortable with the potential military implications of China's growing economic power, despite the great inequalities that remain between China and the Western world.

China's principal interest at this time remains economic, to enhance its access to American and Japanese markets, investment, education, and science and technology. China understands its needs and will not willingly jeopardize that access. For years to come, this is likely to limit Chinese willingness to confront the United States and Japan militarily and politically on some important issues.

China also knows it is by far the weakest of the three and seeks time to grow and strengthen itself. China's traditional international thinking is more rooted in balance-of-power and "Middle

Kingdom" considerations, an intellectual approach that has little currency in Japan or the United States. The divergent views of politics held by China and the United States and Japan create another source of misunderstanding in the relationship. Conceivably, China sees the triangular element as a way of reducing its vulnerability. It may also see forging ties to a post-unification Korea as a way to strengthen its side of the triangle.

Beijing probably worries about U.S. power and intentions most, though there remains considerable emotional hostility and distrust of Japan dating from the colonial era and World War II. Despite Chinese assertions that the United States is a declining power, it does not act as if that were the case, and this position should be viewed as mostly posturing. Anti-American sentiment has been rising in China, partially stimulated by the government; many Chinese seem to believe that elements in the United States are determined to weaken the Chinese political system and ultimately destroy the government. They also believe that only the United States stands between China and resolution of the Taiwan issue.

While distrustful of both countries and ambivalent about the U.S.-Japan alliance, China probably believes the alliance serves as a vehicle for restraining the revival of Japanese militarism. Other Asian countries also believe that this is one effect of the alliance. China may see some possibility of undermining Japanese-American relations by periodically stoking up the Taiwan and Senkaku/Diaoyu issues, but the result of such machinations would be to drive Washington and Tokyo closer together, as was the case with "missile diplomacy" over Taiwan in the spring of 1996. The Chinese government is prepared to invoke the history of Japan's behavior in China to try to obtain concessions from Japan.

China has an interest in loosening the Japanese-American alliance and playing off the two sides economically and diplomatically. It is not clear whether China believes it can really do that.

China has not liked multilateralism as a rule. It mostly seeks independent international standing consistent with its imperial past. China prefers bilateral negotiations, in which it can throw its own weight around, to multilateral ones, in which it may feel as if it has been ganged up on. As the weakest party, China could easily see itself as the odd man out in any trialogue. Beijing will likely be skeptical of the good intentions of Japan and the United States in a trilateral effort.

THE BASIS FOR THREE-WAY DISCUSSION

What can we conclude about the possibilities for and utility of some form of trilateral relationship? Taking each of the three parties' perceptions into account, it would seem that forming any trilateral relationship cannot be a matter of simple geometry. In any case, we are far from even tentative three-way official discussions.

Relations now are bilaterally determined, with some concern for the impact on the third party—the United States and Japan in particular are sensitive to one another's concerns. As the weakest party, China could formulate an approach that would try to make the three-way relationship more equilateral. Beijing would not, however, have confidence it can succeed.

There is no interest in any of the capitals in trying to create a tripartite condominium in Asia. Barring trying to play off one side against the other on an issue-by-issue basis, none of the parties has great enthusiasm for structured trilateral interaction.

China has shown no interest in multilateralizing any of the regional territorial concerns, ranging from Taiwan to the Senkaku/Diaoyu Islands to the South China Sea. That makes trialogue difficult in the security field.

There are, however, potential benefits from and possibilities for a trialogue. In the short run, the greatest benefit of beginning an officially conducted trilateral discussion is to help prevent influential elements in both the United States and Japan from demonizing China. Conceivably, such talks could lead to better insights for all participants on important issues and greater consideration of the impact of policies on one another. A trilateral discussion on an official basis could possibly lead to some useful confidence-building measures and development of common ground in other areas.

Probably the easiest subjects on which to initiate fruitful trilateral discussion are economic and environmental cooperation activities, and in laying out domestic political realities in all three countries. The Senkakus over time could conceivably become a realistic area of trilateral economic cooperation. The Korean peninsula would be an obvious choice in the political/military arena, but China has never shown much interest in Korean talks and may be looking at the peninsula with a much longer time horizon. Taiwan would obviously be an important subject for discussion in order to prevent tensions from escalating—outside of Taiwan it is difficult to develop a scenario where any side would deploy serious force against the other—but China has resisted broader discussion of this issue on grounds that it is a purely domestic matter. Nuclear, missile, and nonproliferation issues would clearly benefit from a three-way discussion, but the United States and Japan should expect China to bring its own equities to the table, i.e., its opposition to ballistic missile defense.

More fundamentally, and at first only on a private-level basis, this trialogue could be used as a way of discussing and perhaps helping diminish long-standing historical and psychological grievances among all the parties, e.g., World War II and the U.S.-Japan alliance. Much would depend on the candor of the discussion. Since it is not possible at this point to deal completely with the concrete tensions among the three, this might provide a fruitful way of developing habits of communication and clearing the ground for more important discussions later.

The benefits from trilateral discussion and possible cooperation on an official basis, however, could be severely reduced by the reaction of other nations left out of the talks, particularly South Korea. Nations of Southeast Asia would notice but might actually applaud the effort as a means of reducing both Chinese and Japanese threats.

At this point, it is not clear—except to those who believe that any discussion will ultimately help reduce distrust and increase transparency—that there are significant benefits to the inauguration of an official trialogue among China, Japan, and the United States. Exploratory, informed, nongovernmental talks would seem well worth pursuing, however, to test the waters. In our age of vast economic growth and increasing international complexity, it would be foolish to accept as axiomatic a static world.

Thinking Trilaterally

Funabashi Yoichi

IN ENGLISH, there is a common saying, "Nature abhors a three-some." Three-person relationships, or triangular relationships, are easily filled with tension. Each partner always eventually suspects that somewhere the two other partners are secretly plotting ways to weaken the third partner. In French, one says, "*Les absents ont toujours tort*," or "The absent ones are always wrong." These facets of human relations are also applicable to international politics.

Compared to bilateral relationships, trilateral relationships are inherently unstable. Three-sided dialogue can easily lead to a swirl of Machiavellian-like interactions. Three-way relations between China, Japan, and the United States are not immune to this pitfall.

Although I speak of a trilateral relationship, in the case of China, Japan, and the United States, relations are asymmetric. Japan and the United States are bound together by an alliance, and this bilateral relationship is deeper than the Sino-U.S. or Sino-Japanese one. Differences in respective political systems, geography, culture, and historical experience also affect interactions among the three countries. Today, even as the importance of constructive dialogue is commonly acknowledged, there has still been almost no preparation toward enhancing mutual understanding or encouraging such dialogue. The three countries are not accustomed to thinking trilaterally, and a culture of dialogue is not being fostered.

Considering the circumstances, describing China-Japan-U.S. relations as "trilateral relations" is almost an exaggeration. It must be admitted that the three nations have not moved beyond their bilateral relations. Yet increasingly each bilateral relationship influences the other bilateral relationships. Avoiding this, or trying to deal with each bilateral relationship separately from the others, is almost completely unworkable. More and more, each bilateral relationship will become ensnared in the trilateral relationship as a whole. Unless a trilateral relationship is created by design, relations among the three nations will become captive to triangular relations created by default.

MUTUAL SUSPICIONS

The cataclysmic changes in the international environment of the 1990s have promoted groundbreaking modification in the structure of interactions among China, Japan, and the United States. The result has been a heightened consciousness of the trilateral relationship.

The major changes of the past ten years include the end of the cold war, the Gulf War, the collapse of the socialist bloc, the appearance of regionalism in Asia Pacific, the rise of China, the democratization of Taiwan, the reaffirmation of the Japan-U.S. alliance, and the possibility of the reunification of the Korean peninsula. China and the United States do not see eye to eye on any of these issues, and Chinese ambivalence about and fear of U.S. motives often are the basis for China's disagreement with U.S. policy.

With the collapse of the Soviet Union and the end of the cold war, the raison d'être for Japanese and American geopolitical cooperation with China, the basis for bilateral ties since the 1970s, evaporated. Without the cohesive force of the perceived Soviet threat, China-U.S. and China-Japan relations faltered. The United States is now the world's sole superpower, and China believes it detects American ambitions to establish a new hegemony. Points of conflict between the two countries that were overlooked during the period when the two followed a common line against the Soviet Union, such as human rights, workers' rights, and the environment, are now suddenly reappearing.

The Clinton administration has succeeded in planning mutual visits of heads of state for 1997 and 1998 and is preaching the logic of "U.S.-China normalization." But the obstacles between the two countries—commonly called the "five T's"—are still relevant and unavoidable. These are Taiwan, trade, Tiananmen (human rights), technology (missile technology exports), and Tibet. China-U.S. relations will, over the long term, undoubtedly continue to be marked by cultural tensions.

Another obstacle to smooth trilateral interaction is the Japanese and American fear that as China becomes a great power, it will attempt to destroy the existing international order by disregarding the norms and standards of international society. In its modern history, Japan has not encountered a China that is powerful economically, politically, and militarily. As China grows into true great power status in Asia Pacific, the sense of rivalry between Japan and China will heighten.

On the other hand, should the Japan-U.S. relationship worsen, this would be a clear incentive for both Japan and China to strive to improve Sino-Japanese relations. For example, during the Japan-U.S. Framework Talks, when Japan-U.S. relations were most tense, Japan and China both responded critically to the domineering attitude of the United States toward human rights and trade issues.

The gradual deepening of Sino-Japanese relations in the trade and economic fields will certainly have an impact on each country's policy toward the United States. Already, Japan is China's largest trading partner. China also is becoming an increasingly important trading partner for Japan. An Australian think tank affiliated with the Australian government predicts that by 2015 China will overtake the United States as Japan's largest trading partner.

Sino-Japanese relations do not at present critically affect Japan-U.S. relations, but this could change as the issues central to Sino-Japanese relations grow more serious. In general, in any nation's process of becoming a great power, nationalism heightens. The "old friends drawing from the same old well" concept of the Sino-Japanese friendship of the 1970s is already withdrawing from the stage. This coolness between the countries began after the Tiananmen Square incident of 1989. More recently, relations were shaken by China's nuclear tests, the Japanese perception of China's increasingly frequent use of "guilt politics" by invoking the war-time history between the two countries, and China's missile tests in the Taiwan Strait crisis of 1996.

China is expressing dissatisfaction with Japan's lack of historical recognition and repentance concerning its accountability for certain actions during World War II. China also has expressed its uneasiness about the prospects of Japan's remilitarization. Chinese leaders have frequently demonstrated their distrust of Japan. That mutual distrust between Japan and China is at a historic high is indicated by many recent opinion polls.

The more Japan feels this "heaviness" (as one high-ranking official of the Ministry of Foreign Affairs called it) in its interactions with China, the more Japan falls prey to the temptation to view the Japan-U.S. alliance as a means to neutralize China. There is gradual, deep-seated change in Japanese policy and politics toward a more aggressive and less cooperative China policy. Experts conclude that Japan's China policy is changing from commercial liberalism to reluctant realism.

For the United States, any worsening of Sino-Japanese relations is not necessarily such a bad thing. Conflict could actually increase U.S. leverage toward both countries, and, therefore, the United States secretly welcomes Sino-Japanese rivalry. Or, at least, such is the suspicion in both China and Japan.

CHINESE CONCERN OVER "CONTAINMENT"

China's biggest concern is that Japan and the United States will agree on a policy of containment toward it. Since the 1970s, China has accepted the Japan-U.S. security alliance as being fundamentally an alliance to combat the Soviet Union, but undoubtedly China also evaluated it as having the hidden function of preventing Japan's reemergence as a great military power. The reaffirmation of the Japan-U.S. Security Treaty announced as the Joint Declaration on Security Cooperation in April 1996, while revising the treaty's character as an anti-Soviet alliance so as to maintain in Asia Pacific a framework for regional stability, did little to assuage China's fear that the purpose of the treaty is to keep China in its place.

Another source of anxiety for China is that the reaffirmation recognizes and promotes Japan's larger political and military role in the region.

The differences of opinion among top party and government officials in China about the reaffirmation are unclear. "Some Chinese officials believe it would be better to try to extinguish the Japan-U.S. Security Treaty, but that is still a minority view. The majority of Chinese officials support the existing status quo," says one researcher at the China Institute for the Study of Current International Relations. Owing to the presence of U.S. troops, mainstream Chinese leaders judge Japan's route to military independence to be contained. In sum, it seems that China is divided into two schools of thought: that the country should recognize the American troop presence and the Security Treaty or that in the long term it should support the withdrawal of American troops so as to undermine the alliance. The backdrop to this policy debate is the Chinese view of America, which also figures prominently in the ongoing debate over China's destiny. Some Chinese officials accuse the United States of denying the country's China containment policy and of concealing its ulterior motive of not recognizing the rise of China.

For Japan, how Sino-U.S. relations develop will be of decisive importance to Japan-U.S. relations. For instance, observers worry about the ricochet effect should Sino-U.S. relations sink to their nadir: it is feared that any chance for the healthy development of an independent Sino-Japanese relationship, free of U.S. influence, would be largely lost. It is also possible that China and the United States will bypass Japan to suddenly improve relations, entering into a honeymoon age. And, as China's process of becoming a truly great power advances, a China-U.S. bipolar system could be born. The possibility then arises that Japan would be excluded from this new bipolar "condominium." But Japan's fear of being ensnared in a China-U.S. confrontation is more acute than that of being excluded from a China-U.S. condominium. Japan's desire to keep its "China option" more autonomous from the United States has traditionally been strong.

Certainly, Japan and the United States have formed an alliance, and China is taking a confrontational stance toward that alliance. But that absolutely does not mean that in trilateral affairs the simplistic diagram of a united Japan and America versus China predominates. After the Clinton administration took office, American policy toward both China and Japan became more tense. One would expect Sino-Japanese relations to have become stronger in response, but they did not. Instead, the degree of tension in Sino-Japanese relations also rose. The fact was that all three bilateral relationships became worse simultaneously.

It is unreasonable to look at the China-Japan-U.S. trilateral relationship as if it were a chess game like the geopolitical triangular relationship of the 1970s between China, the Soviet Union, and the United States. At that time, the strongest power (the United States) and the weakest power (China), in the management of their bilateral relations, deliberately entered into actions that would strongly influence the third power. It seems unlikely that the interaction among China, Japan, and the United States will follow that sort of triangular geopolitical formula. In relations among the three countries today, although the two strongest powers (Japan and America) have formed an alliance, it is not at all designed to confront the third country. The Japan-U.S. alliance was more political than geopolitical in its birth and has continued to maintain that character.

Currently, it is impossible to believe that the Japan-U.S. alliance relationship was reaffirmed in order to name China the "common enemy." Even if the United States were to demand a temporary policy of containment toward China, Japan would oppose it. U.S. insistence on such a policy would undoubtedly have the opposite effect of weakening the Japan-U.S. alliance.

TOWARD STRENGTHENING DIALOGUE

There is room within the trilateral relationship for both conflict and cooperation. Managing their interactions peacefully and constructively is in the long-term interest of all three countries. This is also necessary for the future peace and stability of the Asia Pacific region. Therefore, all three nations need to have the following common understandings regarding the various relations within the region.

First is recognition of the fact that the Japan-U.S. alliance is necessary for the region's stability, both now and increasingly in the future. Recognition implies acknowledging that it is unthinkable that the alliance will view China as an enemy.

Next, various interests and policy intentions should be confirmed for the peace and stability of the Korean peninsula. At the center of this issue are a grasp of shared visions for the region's stability and a common evaluation of Beijing-Tokyo-Washington and Beijing-Seoul-Washington relations, based on the Japan-U.S. Security Treaty and the Korea-U.S. Security Treaty. This problem is of course mainly an issue for the two Korea's, but at the same time subjectively it goes without saying that joint initiatives must also be taken.

China, Japan, and the United States also should heighten the quality of their dialogue and make an effort to forge trilateral relations that create a stable environment. Partners in individual bilateral relationships should make their specific policy intentions and policy trends transparent to the third party. And, to promote trust, bilateral activities should recognize trust strengthening as a goal, and each country must do all it can to see that its bilateral relationships do not advance any policies at the expense of a third country.

As part of the process of strengthening trust, Chinese, Japanese, and U.S. officials should consider the following specific proposals.

All three nations could begin track two consultations by specialist bureaucrats on the economic and security issues that embrace the interests of each, taking care that the viewpoints of each nation are heard.

Efforts should be made to build on the "2 plus 2" dialogues that currently exist between Japan and the United States. These are gatherings at fixed times of foreign policy and defense agency officials from each nation to exchange opinions on foreign policy and security issues. Including Chinese officials from the appropriate ministries for "2 plus 2 plus 2" discussions would represent a big step forward. Because it is predicted that cabinet-level participation would be difficult, the process could be launched with only mid-level officials. To start, perhaps these discussions could begin on the policy planning staff level.

Gradual integration of the currently only bilateral military exchanges into a trilateral system is worthy of consideration. True cooperation among the military forces of all three powers would assure the others of each nation's unassertive intentions.

China, Japan, and the United States should seek to work together at the Asia Pacific Economic Cooperation (APEC) forum. The three countries can and should cooperate in softening trade friction as well as in strengthening APEC's conflict management function. China and Japan need to work cooperatively and persistently to convince the United States, which is currently much less comfortable with the Asia Pacific model of cooperation, to resolve these issues as soon as possible. Their ability to do so can be strengthened by making further contributions of their own to the APEC process.

The success of APEC and the ASEAN Regional Forum (ARF) ultimately depends on actual good relations between Japan and China. Hostility between these two will make unworkable all the multilateral efforts that have recently been so heartening to see in the Asia Pacific region, and ruin any hopes of a true trilateral dialogue.

Japan and the United States should cooperate to facilitate China's attempts to be fully integrated into the international economic system, particularly its accession to the World Trade Organization. All nations must realize the swiftly growing significance of trade and investment between China and Japan. Discounting investment from Taiwan, Hong Kong, and Macao, Japan's foreign investment in China is second only to that of the United States. This rapidly increasing economic interdependence between Japan and China will have far-reaching implications for both Japanese and Chinese foreign policy. As time goes on and trade and investment between the two nations continue to skyrocket, any increase in tension between the two parties will have increasingly negative effects on both nations' economies.

Gradually, the three nations should explore a new mechanism for stabilizing currencies (the U.S. dollar, the Japanese yen, the Hong Kong dollar, and the Chinese renminbi) by coordinating macroeconomic policies. The United States should be encouraged to participate more fully in the emerging new Asia Pacific macroeconomic policy and currency stabilization process.

The promotion of mutual understanding and the strengthening of dialogue in the policy-making process should not be viewed lightly. If there is dialogue among China, Japan, and the United States, possibly through the process of creating a common (three-way) declaration with regard to China's suspicions about the U.S.-Japan Joint Declaration on Security Cooperation, perhaps those suspicions can be allayed somewhat. It is certain that the effort to conduct preliminary dialogue with China before the joint declaration was announced was insufficient.

At the same time, it is also necessary that China be made to understand the meaning of interdependence and peaceful coexistence and the limits and inefficacy of its "Middle Kingdom mentality." For Japan, the lack of Chinese reciprocity in response to the visits to China by the Japanese defense minister and chairman of the Japanese joint chiefs makes it difficult to deepen military exchanges further. Dissatisfaction over this is strong in Japan. The United States also feels China does not play a reciprocal role in the military-to-military exchange program.

The nucleus of the China question is, Can or cannot the international system accept a new great power that is advancing and developing so fast? As long as China is suspicious that the United States, as the dominant existing power, is trying to prevent and/or slow down China's rise, true dialogue with China will be difficult to achieve. Japan and the United States should recognize China as a great power and deal with the country in that manner. In the world as a whole, Japan and the United States should take the lead in accepting China's rise and in welcoming China into international society.

The important role that the Group of Seven (G-7) system played during Japan's ascent serves as a reference. While Japan was becoming an economic great power, the G-7 took various steps to usher Japan into the international economic system. Although there were other elements (the strengthening of relations between Europe and America; the strengthening of Europe's leverage vis-à-vis America; the stability of the dollar; the uniting of the Free World against the Soviet Union, etc.) involved in the launch of the G-7 summit meetings in 1975, one key element was placing Japan into the international system and aiming at a cooperative existence with the country. An approach with a similar framework must also be used for China.

TO BENEFIT ASIA PACIFIC

Developing Asia Pacific regionalism and multilateralism must also be a central goal of Japan-U.S. cooperation. China, Japan, and the United States bear a very large responsibility with regard to the region. Three-way dialogue on regional matters should not be regarded by other Asia Pacific countries as a joint conspiracy, but rather as the three countries shouldering their joint responsibility.

Within the three nations, serious debates are occurring on various proposals for creating a process that aims at strengthening trilateral cooperation and fostering the sort of trilateral relationship that would benefit Asia Pacific. William Perry, American secretary of defense, proposed a meeting of defense ministers from all three nations, but the idea fizzled out at the preliminary policy proposal level. Conversely, the Nixon-Kissinger philosophy that advocates managing Japan and China separately, and thereby increasing leverage with both nations respectively, is especially popular among security specialists in the United States. These specialists do not detect much benefit from advancing trilateral dialogue. Perhaps the United States does not now feel a great need for trilateral dialogue because of its strong independent stances vis-à-vis China and Japan. Another opinion holds that any trilateral dialogue whose aim is to soothe Chinese dissatisfaction regarding the U.S.-Japan security system would instead become a weak point of American policy by functioning as an appeasement of China.

China is aware that it currently is in the weakest position of the three nations. And China is wary of Japan and the United States "collaborating" against it. This is why China is showing interest in trilateral dialogue: trilateralism promises to lessen the strategic importance of China's comparative weakness. Even so, as one of Asia Pacific's three big powers, China may yet hold the conceit that it can perform more skillfully than other countries.

Japan, for now, is still enjoying a privileged status under the terms of the U.S.-Japan security system. Considering China's increasing growth and strength, some observers believe that it would be fruit-ful to organize China-Japan-U.S. dialogue now, while Japan's po-sition is still strong. Others feel that, even if a process of dialogue is created, the present situation of worsening Sino-Japan relations may reduce Japan to no more than a "subcontracting partner" of the United States in any new American game with China. Most Japanese politicians share the view that trilateral dialogue can only proceed effectively once China and Japan have become close friends. In contrast, others are concerned that starting a China-Japan-U.S. dialogue will weaken the unique relationship that Japan and the United States enjoy through their alliance, and that any tri-lateral dialogue might eventually end up lending a hand to China's perceived policy of separating the United States and Japan.

Despite the many obstacles to China-Japan-U.S. dialogue, con-structive trilateral interaction is one of three keys that are needed to create stability and trustworthiness in the Asia Pacific region.

The first key is strengthening commitment to APEC. APEC is the one existing great hope for true multilateral engagement in the whole Asia Pacific region. APEC gives East Asian nations, particu-larly China, which until a decade ago was isolated, a chance to en-hance cooperative working relationships and to create a milieu within which more multilateral and regional dialogue can be pro-moted. Additionally, APEC serves the vital purpose of keeping the United States engaged in the region.

The second key is the continuing security alliance between Japan and the United States. The U.S.-Japan security alliance has greatly contributed to stability in the whole region. It allowed the United States to maintain a forward presence to contain the Soviet threat while, perhaps no less important, reassuring countries in the re-gion against any possible reemergence of Japanese imperialism. An end to or a weakening of this alliance would drastically shake East Asian nations' confidence and belief in an open, liberal sys-tem. It would mean that the United States had withdrawn its cover, and it would also signify to most a resurgence of Japanese power, which would have to be matched. Most importantly, it would mean an end to the security system under which East Asia has seen the most impressive economic growth in its history. For smaller countries in the region, continuance of the alliance will be "a golden way to ensure that the hegemonism of both Japan and China can be contained and balanced out," according to one Singaporean diplomat. Japan and the United States must retain their close ties even while seeking to strengthen a multilateral security system, or else East Asians will see multilateralism as a disguise for U.S. withdrawal from the region and an unavoidable clash between Japan and China for hegemony.

The third key is trilateral dialogue between Japan, China, and the United States. The three countries must cooperate so that a stable balance can be achieved in East Asia. Cooperation among these three major powers will be more crucial to the stability of the Korean peninsula in the next three to five years. The accommodative initiative of the United States toward North Korea in the past three years and its delicate balance among the concerned parties could be upset if North Korea's new leadership revises its U.S.-focused policy and explores the possibility of new ties with China and Japan.

Each nation tends to be culturally arrogant and has certain constraints, but each nation must see that cooperation is the more attractive option. Japan and the United States must swiftly include China in their deliberations and achieve trilateral cooperation, or else China will see the Japan-U.S. alliance as a force for containment instead of constancy. Conversely, China might attempt to use its growing market to induce competition and distrust between Japan and the United States through preferential economic treatment. Japan and the United States must cooperate so that Chinese leaders who believe in employing the old Chinese method of "using barbarians to fight barbarians" do not succeed in using economic favoritism to break the alliance.

Stability in Asia Pacific could be viewed as a building. Between the solid foundation of the bipolar Japan-U.S. alliance and the roof of the multilateral structures represented by ARF and APEC, there is room for another pillar. This pillar could be the trilateral structure of China-Japan-U.S. dialogue.

With this pillar, the soundness of regional stability would greatly increase. If we can create that kind of strong structure, it will be useful for adapting to all the different types of power game shocks that will be born in the region in this, the age of Asian great powers.

Trilateral dialogue will serve to create a stable balance in the region that will be in the long-term national interest of all three nations.

China-Japan-U.S. dialogue is expected to include the important strategic values that will advance Japan's national interests in the long term. Through trilateral dialogue, Japan can maintain its security ties to the United States while allowing Sino-Japanese relations to deepen and mature. Japan must make sure that these two objectives do not come into conflict. Japan can defend itself simultaneously against its paradoxical foreign relations nightmares: China-U.S. confrontation, which would lead to Japan being caught in the middle, and China-U.S. romance, which would leave Japan isolated.

After World War II, Japan experienced both of these nightmares, due to first the anti-China foreign policy of John Foster Dulles and then the Nixon-Kissinger détente with China. For Japan, there is a need to apply a minimum brake on any similar sudden change in China-U.S. diplomacy. For the future, even supposing that China and the United States form a "bipolar age," Japan will be able to place itself in the middle if the trilateral process and mechanism are firmly constructed.

Japan and the United States need to pull China into a dialogue in order to continue to maintain the Japan-U.S. relationship without imposing on China or viewing China as an enemy. Firmly established trilateral relations could become the umbrella that would guarantee the protection of the U.S.-Japan security alliance.

More so for Japan than for China and the United States, three-way dialogue contains an awareness not only of national prosperity but also maybe of survival strategy. If Japan is acutely sensitive and prepared, perhaps it could achieve the reflex of thinking trilaterally. Japan should make decisions regarding its long-term interest on the basis of a trilateral context. The right path for Japan is to advance both its foreign policy toward China and the United States and its foreign policy toward the region toward the realization of such a trilateral context. Through quiet diplomacy and subtle overtures, Japan can make use of the right time—right now—to achieve trilateral dialogue.

Wasn't it Japan's forefathers of the Meiji era who referred to that sort of thinking as "Sino-Japanese-Western" (*wakanyou*) fusion? To be able to achieve some sort of workable trilateral dialogue and policy coordination, the policymakers of all three nations must first make an effort to learn about the other two. Being aware of each country's national interests, studying their culture and language, learning their historical perspectives, and pursuing true economic and educational cooperation are all necessary for it to become a habit for the policymakers of all three nations to be able to truly think trilaterally.

Contributors

MORTON I. ABRAMOWITZ, Senior Fellow, Council on Foreign
Relations

FUNABASHI YOICHI, Chief Diplomatic Correspondent and Columnist for the *Asahi Shimbun*

WANG JISI, Director, Institute of American Studies, Chinese
Academy of Social Sciences

The Japan Center for International Exchange

FOUNDED IN 1970, the Japan Center for International Exchange (JCIE) is an independent, nonprofit, and nonpartisan organization dedicated to strengthening Japan's role in international affairs. JCIE believes that Japan faces a major challenge in augmenting its positive contributions to the international community, in keeping with its position as one of the world's largest industrial democracies. Operating in a country where policy-making has traditionally been dominated by the government bureaucracy, JCIE has played an important role in broadening debate on Japan's international responsibilities by conducting international and cross-sectional programs of exchange, research, and discussion.

JCIE creates opportunities for informed policy discussions; it does not take policy positions. JCIE programs are carried out with the collaboration and cosponsorship of many organizations. The contacts developed through these working relationships are crucial to JCIE's efforts to increase the number of Japanese from the private sector engaged in meaningful policy research and dialogue with overseas counterparts.

JCIE receives no government subsidies; rather, funding comes from private foundation grants, corporate contributions, and contracts.

DATE DUE

NO 21 '98			
DE 1 8 '98			

DEMCO 38-297